The Crusades

On a chill November day in 1095, Pope Urban II stepped out onto a rickety platform above the streets of Clermont in France, and addressed the crowd: "The Anti-Christ is at hand! Until now you have been slaying each other just out of greed or pride. Now we call on you to fight the wicked Infidel and win glorious martyrdom."

Thus began a great Holy War. For nearly two hundred years, the Christians of Western Europe battled to win back the Holy Lands of Palestine from Saracen hands. They rode and marched in their thousands, noble knights and humble peasants, rich people and poor, old men and children. And, coming home, they brought with them tales of the wondrous East, and new standards to live for.

In this lavishly-illustrated book, the author tells the exciting story of sieges and slaughter, of Richard the Lion Heart and the noble Saladin, and explains the impact of the Crusades on the future of Europe.

A WAYLAND SENTINEL BOOK

The Crusades

Matthew Holden

"God wills it!"
  Crusaders' rallying cry.

WAYLAND PUBLISHERS LONDON

More Sentinel Books

Frontispiece: The English, French and German armies lay siege to Damascus (from a fifteenth century manuscript).

SBN 85340 218 3
Copyright © 1973 by Wayland (Publishers) Limited
101 Grays Inn Road, London WC1
Set in 'Monophoto' Baskerville and
printed offset litho in Great Britain by
Page Bros (Norwich) Ltd, Norwich

Contents

List of Illustrations

1. "God wills it!"

Few events in history evoke more romantic images than the Crusades. These expeditions to the Holy Land shine like sparkling jewels from the dreary drabness of the Dark Ages. To the Crusades is credited the beginning of the modern age -- the birth of today's world; and also a mass of legends, heroic tales, knightly feats and mythical bravery.

The declared purpose of the Crusades was to drive the infidel Moslems, known as Saracens, from Jesus Christ's homeland. Christians from all the countries of western Europe banded together. Their leaders were princes and knights, and they marched under the banner of the Church to liberate the Holy Land -- modern Palestine.

Priests preached from their pulpits to the eager masses. Peasants flocked from their humble homes, and barons rode out from their castles, to join God's army and drive the heathens from Jerusalem. They were sure the barbarians would flee before such a holy host.

But this noble aim does not tell the whole story of the Crusades. Romance has clouded reality. Many of those who crusaded did so for political purposes, or for greed, or for mere delight in slaughter. The Christians could be as cruel as their enemy. Bravery indeed was common, but so too was brutality. The Crusades were full of horror as well as glory.

Right The people of Europe joined together under the banner of the Christian church to drive the Saracens from the Holy Land.

8

Declaration of war

A gaunt, hollow-eyed figure steps onto a rickety platform in the chill streets of Clermont, France. Below him, cramming the narrow alleyways, are jostling pilgrims, peasant, merchants, adventurers and knights. The crowd cheers when the thin figure, dressed in sumptuous robes, comes into sight. "The Pope. See – the Pope!" they shout.

Seven months before, fresh appeals had come from the Middle East for help in driving the Saracens from the Holy Land. Simultaneously, a tremendous and terrifying shower of meteorites had fallen from the heavens. The Church looked upon the meteorites as a sign from God – act now or the Devil, known then as "Anti-Christ," will conquer the world.

So, on this wintry November day in 1095, Pope Urban II raises his hands and the tumult dies. He plays first upon the fears of the peasants.

"The end of the world is near. The days of Anti-Christ are at hand. If, when he comes, he finds no Christians in the East, as at this moment there are none, then truly will there be no man to stand up against him."

He then turns his attention to the barons and powerful lords. "Until now, you have been slaying each other just out of greed or pride, whereby you have earned everlasting death. Now we call on you to fight the wicked Infidel and win glorious martyrdom."

A Holy War must be initiated – all who fight will be pardoned past sins, and all who die will be martyrs. Christ's army will gather at Constantinople, and from there strike south against the evil Saracens.

Pope Urban's declaration at Clermont brings

Above Pope Urban II, who launched the First Crusade.

immediate and tremendous relief to his apprehensive audience. Men shout and cheer, and a mighty cry of *"Dieu le volt!"* ("God wills it!") echoes through the sodden streets.

The Pope's message spreads rapidly throughout western Europe. It is carried by priests, travellers and merchants – and by Peter the Hermit, a native of Amiens, wandering barefoot in a dirty linen smock, with shaggy hair, and staring, half-mad eyes.

Below The Pope, in the market-place at Clermont, urges the excited throng around him to launch a Holy War against the Infidel.

Romance

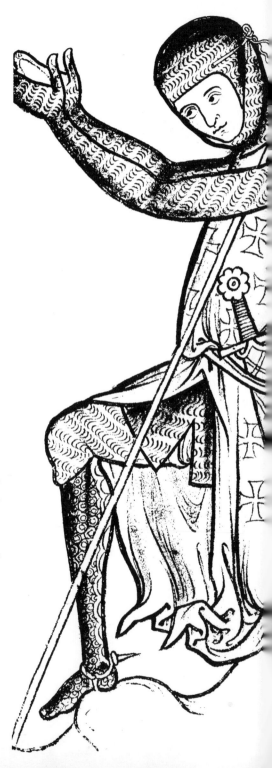

Yet even before the First Crusade set out, romance had already begun to conceal reality. Appeals for help in driving out the Saracens had reached the Pope before, and they had always been ignored. This time the call was being answered – but only because it now suited Urban's political ambitions. He fervently wished to increase his power and influence, and to extend his own kingdom; and he would use the Crusades to bring this about.

The romance which surrounds the Crusades has grown up through the centuries, with the help of popular ballads, heroic poems and the stories of boastful Crusaders. Battles were apparently exciting affairs, fought by pious men full of honour and courage. This contemporary account is typical of the romantic view of the Crusades.

"Then you might have seen many a banner and pennon of various shapes floating in the breeze; people of various nations, arms of various kinds, helmets with crests and brilliant with jewels, shining

Left Romance paints a picture
of the Crusader as chivalrous,
honourable and bold. Here a
knight kneels humbly in
prayer before leaving to fight.

mail and shields emblazoned with lions or flying
dragons in gold; mules and horses, eager to move at
full speed and burning with indignation at being
held by the foaming bit; many a lance with its sharp
point glittering; the air sparkling with the gleaming
of swords, and so many soldiers, choice men, good
and true."

Romance also gives the leaders of the Crusades a
saint-like aura. According to legend, Richard I, the
Lionheart, was kind and honourable and fought
gloriously for God in the Holy Land. One of his
ardent followers wrote: "He was far superior to all
others, both in moral goodness and in strength, and
memorable for prowess in battle, where his mighty
deeds outshone the most brilliant description we
could give of them."

Not only Richard, but also his subordinates,
seemed to possess superhuman endurance and
courage. The Saracens on the other hand were
brutal, evil and base – or so say the legends.

Reality

Richard I had as many faults as virtues. During the ten years that he was King of England, he spent barely six months in his realm. And many were the heavy and unjust taxes he imposed on his subjects in order to finance his foreign adventures. He thought nothing of selling his royal possessions, which he would then re-possess and sell again when he had a better offer. And his enjoyment of fighting amounted to an obsession. He could be treacherous as well as honourable, and extremely cruel as well as gentle.

The Saracens were known for their methods of torture, and delighted in severing Crusader heads as trophies. The Mongols, who fought during the later Crusade period, could behave in even more fearful fashion -- one captured prince, al-Kamil, was forced to eat his own flesh, slice by slice, until death relieved him of his task.

Yet the Crusaders were a match for them, cruelty for cruelty. Even before the First Crusade had reached the Holy Land, its members had spread terror through southern Europe by pillage and destruction. One town, in modern Bulgaria, attempted some defence against the unruly horde. "Wherefore, we set fire to it," wrote a chronicler, "and burned the town with all that dwelt therein." And when this First Crusade succeeded in taking Jerusalem, the "noble" knights went mad in their enjoyment of slaughter. Men, women and children were hacked to pieces, until the whole city was full of Saracen corpses.

Crusaders were quite capable of behaving like savages. They even ate human meat. Peter the Hermit is said to have commented: "Do you not see

Below Fighting during the Crusades was savage and brutal, and the so-called "Christian" soldiers ruthlessly slaughtered hundreds of men, women and children.

these dead Turks? They are excellent food." And one document described the French Crusaders as "loving Turk flesh better than spiced peacock."

Romance would reject the idea of a Crusader gnawing at a human bone. Nor would it depict Richard the Lionheart riding proudly back to camp with a dozen dripping Saracen heads dangling from his saddle – yet he delighted in doing so.

Battle area

To understand the Crusades, it is necessary to appreciate not merely the religious appeal of the Holy Lands, but the commercial and political attraction of the whole Mediterranean area.

This is the region called "the cradle of civilization." For centuries, while Britain and northern Europe slumbered, the Mediterranean had prospered. The shores were rich in raw materials and trade goods – oil and wine from Sicily, honey from Corsica, lead and iron from Sardinia, wheat and cotton from Egypt, and iron, copper, tin, silver, cattle and slaves from a multitude of other ports.

Civilizations had flourished and declined there. The Cretans, Assyrians, Carthaginians, Greeks and Persians had all come and gone in the Mediterranean area. Finally the great power of Rome, which stretched in A.D. 117 to Britain, France, parts of Germany, Spain, Italy, most of central Europe, Greece, Asia Minor, the Holy Land, Egypt and North Africa, was brought down by internal quarrels and barbarian attacks from the East.

Two developments resulted from the eclipse of Rome. Firstly, Rome itself became of secondary importance to the city of Constantinople, today called Istanbul, which had been established by the Roman Emperor Constantine. This city became the centre of the great Byzantine Empire. Secondly, a barrier fell between northern Europe and the Mediterranean. The Roman conquest had linked the two worlds – now they became separate again.

So, while the Mediterranean continued to seethe with activity in the hot sunshine, and Constantinople grew ever more splendid under the Byzantine influence, northern Europe fell into the silence of the

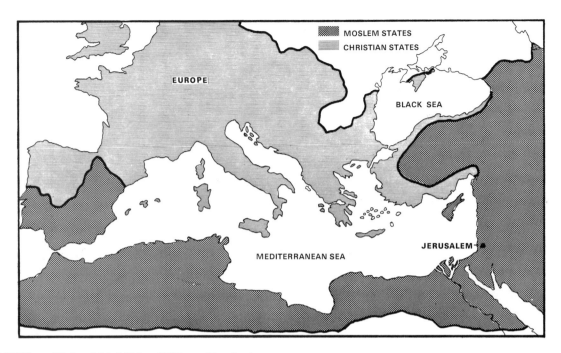

MOSLEM STATES
CHRISTIAN STATES

EUROPE

BLACK SEA

JERUSALEM

MEDITERRANEAN SEA

Dark Ages.

Occasionally, news and strange reports reached the drab, wet, northern regions from the mysterious East – tales of vast riches, strange customs and glittering cities of gold. And one link always remained strong. Jesus Christ had been born in Bethlehem, and crucified in Jerusalem – and these two sacred places in Palestine formed the heart of the Christian religion. Far away they may have been, but they remained nonetheless precious.

Above Moslem and Christian areas of influence at the time of the First Crusade.
Left Constantinople, the capital of the Byzantine empire, was famous for its wealth and splendour.

used by Church as reason for Crusade

17

Moslems

A young Arab led a plodding camel train through the scorching, shimmering desert. He was alone with his thoughts in the searing desolation, and his thoughts centred upon the idea of God. The man was Mohammed, born 570 years after Christ. And his solitary thoughts gave birth to the Moslem religion.

Mohammed, who could probably neither read nor write, had simple ideas about worship. He believed in a God who preached virtue. He believed in a heaven, and in a hell for sinners. He admitted there may have been prophets before him, such as Jesus and Moses, but he became convinced that he himself had been chosen to complete God's new preaching.

Mohammed rejected the complicated trappings which had grown up around orthodox Christianity – the Holy Trinity, the Incarnation, and the Sacraments. His teaching, like Mohammed himself, was straightforward and easy to understand.

His religion came to be called "Islam" – "The Right Way" – and those who agreed with his ideas were known as "The True Believers," or Moslems. They were also called Mohammedans, and grew rapidly in number amongst the Arab tribes.

Believers spread the new religion by peaceful conversion and also by conquest. Gradually, Islam seeped through Syria, Egypt, North Africa and most of Spain. But pockets of Christianity continued to survive, even in the heart of the Arab Moslem world. Above all, Constantinople remained faithful to the Christian faith, despite a gradual shrinking of the Byzantine Empire.

The Byzantine form of Christianity, however,

Below Mohammed, the founder of "Islam," spread his teaching by conquest as well as by peaceful conversion.

began increasingly to differ from that laid down by Popes in the West. The western Popes now had two rivals -- the Moslem religion, and the Byzantine form of Christianity. Appeals for help from Constantinople, threatened by the Turkish Moslems, were for a long time ignored. The Popes hoped that one rival would wipe out the other, and that in the confusion papal power would be restored.

But now, at the famous Council of Clermont in 1095, Pope Urban had judged that the time had come for Crusading intervention in the East.

Twyllyam

Religion and royalty

Pope Urban's aims were as much concerned with politics as with religion. Jerusalem had been taken over by the Moslems as early as A.D. 638. The early occupiers were tolerant towards the Christian inhabitants of the city. Then, in 1076, Jerusalem had come under the control of the fierce Seljuk Turks. They were renowned for their cruelty, and immediately began to slaughter the small pockets of Christians in the Holy Land. Gradually, the Turks began to spread north towards Constantinople, and the Byzantine Emperor, Alexius Comnenus, repeatedly appealed to the Pope for help.

Pope Urban realized that if he graciously gave assistance, and the Crusade emerged successful, he could claim to be overall Christian leader in both East and West. Moreover, he felt that a Crusade would unite a divided Europe behind him.

Far greater unity existed in Britain at this time than anywhere else in Europe. This British unity was largely due to William the Conqueror, who, after his successful invasion in 1066, had exerted his power

Left William the Conqueror. This Norman king was ruthless and efficient, and ruled over his new kingdom with a firm hand.

over the land with ruthless efficiency. Thousands of people were slaughtered or starved to death, and thousands became virtual slaves to the Norman barons.

These barons were themselves kept under strict control by William. Each of them only enjoyed his possessions by courtesy of the Crown, who could take them away at the slightest provocation. Hence a feudal unity was achieved.

Nor did William allow the Church to be independent. He appointed his own man, Lanfranc, as Archbishop of Canterbury, and all major Church decisions had to receive royal approval.

Pope Urban, through his call for a Crusade, hoped to reassert his papal authority. William had died in France in 1087, after being wounded in battle. His son, Rufus, was universally hated and it was possible that the Church might gain support at his expense.

This, then, was the political background to the "religious" Crusades.

The nobility

Nowhere does romance cloud reality more obviously than in the vision of the "noble knight," riding so gaily and gloriously to the First Crusade. In fact knights were uncouth and illiterate, and many were no more than thugs.

Names such as "lord," "baron" and "earl" are confusing, and had comparatively little meaning at the time of the First Crusade. Baron and lord were not titles of honour, but were merely used to describe someone who controlled an area of land on behalf of the King.

The most senior noblemen, who controlled whole counties, were termed earls by William the Conqueror. He made sure that they were all of loyal Norman blood. The King, therefore, owned all the land and all that grew upon it. Everyone, even the most senior nobleman, lived in his constant service.

The great majority of "nobles" were simply landlords of one or two villages, no more than hamlets by today's standards. The nobles were often poverty-stricken. Their houses were little better than the hovels of their peasants, and, like their peasants, they suffered frequently from starvation.

All barons, lords and earls were obliged to fight on behalf of the King. If he ordered them to take part in a Crusade, then they had to go -- whether or not they were filled with religious enthusiasm.

And as for the knights, many were not noblemen at all. At the time of the First Crusade, ideas of knightly honour and chivalry, as described in the legends of the knights of the Round Table, had still to be formulated.

In fact, the Crusades themselves helped to create these chivalrous principles. But, at the time of Pope

Below Few Crusader knights were noble or honourable. Most of them were greedy uncouth thugs, who travelled to the Holy Land in search of excitement, war, booty, and plunder.

Urban's appeal, knights lived for war and rarely for anything else. A plan to rescue a damsel in distress would have been met with incredulous stares, followed by coarse hilarity. The plan to rescue Jerusalem from the Turks was attractive – but more for the promise of bloody battles, plunder and booty than for the promise of Christian salvation.

The people

Romance has treated the knights with too much kindness. The ordinary foot-soldiers on the other hand, are generally overlooked. Yet these humble ranking soldiers provided the bulk of the manpower for the Crusades, even though they played a subservient role to the knights in battle. The knights had obvious reasons for starting on the Crusades -- the search for glory and loot. But what could the simple infantryman hope to gain?

First and most important, by journeying on a Crusade, the peasant could escape his deplorable

Life was hard for the peasants of England under their new Norman masters. But the Crusades offered a means of escape from the daily drudgery of fishing (*left*) or ploughing (*below*).

existence at home. No romance can possibly be attached to the lives led by the ordinary people during those troubled times.

Life had become increasingly hard in England since the Norman conquest. William's henchmen had thrown out the existing landowners, and tenants were now bound to the land and to the lord who controlled it in a way which differed little from slavery.

A tenant rented a small piece of land, and in return was bound to his lord. He could not journey from his lord's estate without permission, and he had to till, cultivate and harvest his lord's estate as well as finding time to look after his own land, upon which he relied for his food. He had to share his harvest with his master, handing over two sheaves of wheat in every ten.

The lord could do virtually as he pleased with his tenants and their children. However brutal or callous his behaviour, there was little they could do in reply. Courts in England were run by Norman judges, following Norman laws. Most of the senior noblemen were also Norman. Those who were not of Norman blood, therefore, had an especially difficult time. And a tenant who turned against his master could expect terrible punishment, both for himself and for his family. Everyday life for the ordinary people was filled with drudgery and fear.

Harsh times

Rolf lives in the south of England. He is fourteen. His father is tenant of a few acres of land, mostly rough scrub, owned by a minor lord who controls two villages, this one and another three miles away.

Rolf's home is a two-room building, built out of turf and with a leaky thatched roof. Like his mother and father and four brothers, Rolf wears ragged clothes and is covered with lice and fleas. He has never had a bath. The lord of the village is almost as dirty. He lives just up the track, in a wooden house dripping with damp.

Rolf's food consists of gruel made from beans and herbs, with weak barley beer to wash it down. Meat is scarce. Rolf's family might have a dish of strong salted beef once a fortnight, and they are allowed a scraggy goose at Michaelmas and a roast pig for Christmas. Famines sweep the countryside about once every ten years. Rolf can still remember the last one – everybody, including the local lord, was forced to eat acorns and soup made from grass. Hundreds of people died of starvation. Medical treatment is crude, restricted to such remedies as broth made from human brains and ant eggs, and ointments culled from mashed worms, cobwebs and woodlice.

Rolf and his family fall into their rough beds at sunset, and rise before dawn. Entertainment is virtually unknown, except for occasional bear-baiting and brutish all-in wrestling.

Once, however, Rolf saw a tournament. He will always remember the spectacle of knights charging against each other in mock combat, their lances lowered, their horses thundering across the turf.

Left Jousting was the sport of the rich, and tournaments were very popular in medieval times.

Rolf can never hope for more than his grim daily routine. Education is impossible. His father would like to send him to a nearby monastery where he would be taught to read and write. But, to make up for the loss of labour caused by Rolf's absence, his lord would demand a large sum of money. This is out of the question.

Then comes a momentous day. Rolf hears that a Crusade is being organized and that his lord needs another servant to take with him.

2. Beginnings

Rolf and his family, and noblemen and peasants living in their dirty hovels throughout northern Europe, consider the Saracens to be uncivilized. They know little of the exotic foods, the high degree of learning, and the delicate and effective medicines enjoyed by their enemy.

Yet, despite this ignorance, tales of the mysterious East tantalized northern listeners. The Saracens might still be unknown to them, but travellers to the Christian outpost of Constantinople brought back tales of a wondrous city – luxurious mansions, colonnaded walks, drainage systems and scented gardens. And these rumours filter back even to Rolf's forgotten village.

Below The people of northern Europe knew little about the mysterious East, but travellers to Constantinople brought back tales of a wonderful and exciting city.

Above Rolf and his friends would never have believed that the city of Constantinople had an efficient drainage system and vast water reservoirs.

Now Rolf has the chance to see all these marvels for himself. Indeed, Pope Urban has given every peasant an opportunity to escape from his grim routine. The Church has appealed for recruits for the Crusade. If a lord prevents a peasant from enlisting in the army, he is challenging not only the will of the Pope, but the will of God himself.

Rolf, and thousands of others like him, can exchange the terrible daily toil at home for a different kind of labour, far overseas – a labour which promises release from the slavery of serfdom, and, for the nobles, riches beyond comprehension.

Pope Urban's appeal has meant that life will never be the same again, neither for those who leave to embark upon the Crusades, nor even for those who remain at home. Northern Europe is once more linked to the south, and the sun.

Recruitment

One of the most astounding features of the whole saga of the Crusades was the enthusiastic response to Pope Urban's first appeal in 1095. His message spread far and wide. And everywhere people answered the call, with goods, money or their services.

One reason for this was the licence which the Pope gave for people to throw off the yoke of slavery and fight for Christ. He had also declared that all

Crusaders, great or small, would be forgiven their past sins. Tempted by this promise and a strong desire to see the marvels of the East, people flocked forth from their stinking hovels.

Only a small percentage in fact went on the Crusades for the real, declared reason – religion. But these few, mainly priests, cloaked the whole enterprise with a heady mixture of religious fervour and saint-like purpose. "God wills it!" they cried.

And this rallying call rang throughout Italy, the Rhine Valley, the upper Danube, France and the Netherlands, Scandinavia, Spain and Portugal. The echo, slightly harder to hear, reached across the Channel into the England of William Rufus, and penetrated even as far as Scotland.

The most active area for the first movement to the Holy Land was what is now France. One contemporary writer, Abbot Cuibert of Nogent, reported: "Each pilgrim was so bent on raising money, come what may, that he parted with his goods, not at his own price but at the buyer's." This process brought a situation bordering on chaos. Normal trade fell into confusion as people sold off their belongings as fast as they could.

Those reluctant to join the Crusades were "persuaded" by their neighbours. "Several people sent a present of a distaff (a spinning stick) to one another," wrote an eye-witness to this upheaval, "as a hint that whosoever declined the campaign would degrade himself as much as if he did the duties of a woman. Wives urged their husbands, mothers their sons, to devote themselves to this noble contest."

Peter the Hermit

Peter left his hermit's existence in a cave near Amiens to travel the highways and byways spreading Pope Urban's message. His weird appearance, his impassioned words and his strange behaviour had tremendous impact on those who saw him.

Soon, Peter had an enormous following. People plucked hairs from the tail of his mule to keep as holy relics. Everywhere in northern France, men put down their tools and left their ploughs to "take up the Cross." Abbot Cuibert wrote that it became common to see peasants trundling with their families, eastwards on oxen-carts. Behind them, the fields lay deserted, and whole towns fell into empty silence.

Pope Urban, speaking at the famous Clermont meeting in November, 1095, had said that the First Crusade should start on 15th August, 1096, after the harvests had been gathered. But so great was the enthusiasm, and so powerful the teaching of Peter the Hermit and of the German monk, Gottschalk, that the peasants began their own Crusade months before the appointed time. Peter himself led the way.

Left Peter the Hermit preached fiery sermons to the people of France, urging them to "take up the Cross" and follow him to the Holy Land.

Thus began the so-called "People's Crusade." With Peter the Hermit went Gottschalk, a knight called Sir Walter the Penniless, and over forty thousand men, women and children. They grossly outnumbered the eighteen thousand foot-soldiers who made up the army. The whole scheme was doomed to disaster. The peasants had no idea of the distance to be covered, nor of the difficulties involved. And they had totally insufficient food, finance and clothing. Most of them had no real idea why they were there in the first place. And, on the difficult journey south through Europe, the leaders started to lose control.

Some of the Crusaders turned upon the Jews, considering them as much heathen as the Moslem Saracens. Increasingly large numbers of innocent Jews were murdered – at Verdun, Trèves, Mainz, Speyer and Worms. And, in Cologne, as many as ten thousand were massacred during several days of terrible slaughter. Such was the Christian behaviour of these holy pilgrims.

33

The People's Crusade

Only about a third of those who had started out on the People's Crusade managed to stagger into Constantinople. From there, they advanced raggedly into the lands of the grim Seljuk Turks. As soon as they had crossed the Bosphorus, they quarrelled amongst themselves. The French members of the Crusade separated from the Germans, the Lombards and the Italians, and marched on alone towards the Turkish kingdom of Roum.

Meanwhile, the second column approached the castle of Exorogorgon, which to their delight seemed empty. The peasants swarmed inside, straight into the trap which the cunning Turks had set. The enemy immediately surrounded the castle and the town. They had run the wells dry before allowing the Christians in, and soon the peasants began to suffer terrible agonies from thirst.

After eight days of extreme hardship and suffering, the peasant leader, Rainald, slipped out from the city to surrender, asking in return that he himself should be spared. The Turks agreed to this treachery, and the massacre inside the town began. Some peasants were beheaded on the spot, others were used as targets for archery practice, and many were sold into fearful slavery.

The French column, which had split from the rest earlier, also ran into trouble. Peter the Hermit became so disgusted with the behaviour of his rabble that he had returned to Constantinople, leaving the leadership to Walter the Penniless.

Believing that only the prospect of battle would restore order among such an ill-disciplined mob, Sir Walter led his men deeper and deeper into Saracen territory. But the wily Turks had once again

made skilful preparations. The French were ambushed. And, in the short battle which followed, Sir Walter and seventeen thousand peasants were slaughtered. The rest fled, to be hunted down and beheaded, or to die of starvation in the wilderness.

So ended the People's Crusade. Meanwhile, however, a far more effective expedition was being prepared. This venture, known officially as the First Crusade, had been organized for full-scale war. And journeying to Cologne, where the Crusaders were to gather, was the lord of Rolf's village, and Rolf himself.

Below The People's Crusade lacked organization and discipline, and only a few of the peasants who set out for the Holy Land ever returned to Europe.

The Christian army

Rolf and two other boy servants had first travelled with their lord to the south coast of England. There they had boarded a small, smelly fishing boat, which had taken them and another knight across to France. Travelling along the dusty roads towards Cologne, they had fallen in with an increasing number of horsemen, servants, foot-soldiers and civilians. Roads became crowded with a seething, shouting, confused mass. This chaotic host formed the basis of the army for the First Crusade.

Christian armies which took part in the Crusades were organized on very different lines from those of today. They had no real discipline, and systems of command were haphazard. A great lord took with him a certain number of soldiers, depending on how powerful he was. Some would be infantry, others cavalry. Many of those whom Rolf met on the roads through France, for example, belonged to Lord Baldwin of Boulogne, who was taking with him five hundred armed knights, and two thousand men on foot.

Each lord was bound by allegiance to a more senior nobleman, but this allegiance was usually loose and flexible. The small noble, for instance, had to serve for forty days with his overlord, but after this period he was free to leave for home or serve under another lord. If a particular commander seemed more successful than others, smaller lords would flock to join his army, and vice versa. Each leader, small or large, had to provide for the men under him. The richer a lord, the more men he would attract to join his unit.

Crusading armies were composed of two kinds of

forces. One, the smaller proportion, was made up of large units brought by the most powerful nobles, which remained in his direct service. But there was also a great mass of small, individual units which were under the command of the lesser nobles. Many, like Rolf's master, had brought only their own servants with them. Others commanded a handful of foot-soldiers. And more still were simple adventurers who had grouped a score of people around them.

For these lesser knights, loyalty depended upon personal whims, a system common to most medieval armies. But the Crusading forces had one unusual feature, which Rolf found very obvious as he trudged along the crammed French roads. A great number of non-fighting people had also attached themselves to the Crusade armies. These civilians were mostly poor and ill-prepared, and were a serious burden for the already hard-pressed Crusaders.

Left A knight and his small group of retainers were a self-contained unit in the Crusader army.

The knights

Like the vast majority of his companions, Rolf knew virtually nothing about warfare. Even though he might have to fight, as a foot-soldier he had received no training, and would probably receive only minimum instruction before battle.

Left The Crusader knight was well-armed and well-protected. He carried a sword and shield and wore chain mail and a strong helmet (*right*). Later helmets became more elaborate and covered the entire face and neck (*below*).

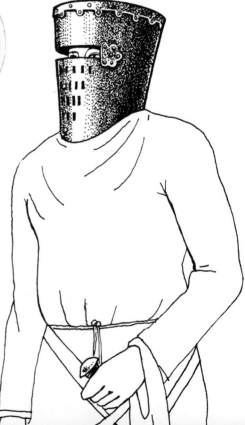

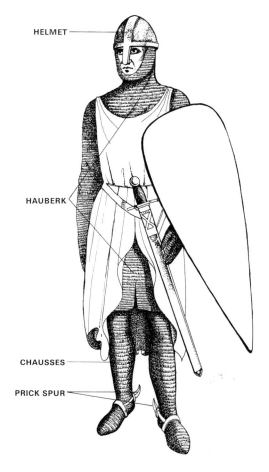

HELMET

HAUBERK

CHAUSSES

PRICK SPUR

Knights, although less numerous than the infantry, received all the glory and all the honour. These horsemen were armed with lances for the initial clash with the enemy, swords for close combat, and daggers for hand-to-hand fighting. They also carried kite-shaped shields on their left arms.

Their lances were long, sometimes over ten feet, with specially-hardened tips. Swords had become heavier and larger during the decades before the First Crusade – so much so that Rolf could hardly lift one even using two hands. These mighty swords were too heavy for thrusting and parrying; instead, they were slashed downwards as gigantic cutting weapons.

Plate armour had not yet been invented, and Rolf's lord wore a long coat of close-woven steel rings, called "mail" (from the French word for mesh). This coat, or hauberk, reached down to the knees, and sometimes even the calfs. Beneath it were leg pieces of the same material, or thick linen stockings, "chausses," which were cross-gartered with leather thongs.

Helmets had recently been improved. The piece which projected down to protect the nose had been lengthened and strengthened. Armourers even provided helmets which covered the entire head and neck. Helmets of this kind were much too heavy to wear for very long, and were usually carried on the pommel of the saddle until action began. Even the smaller "pot" helmets weighed over ten pounds.

Weight was indeed the knight's main problem, since chain mail suits could weigh as much as forty pounds. Cavalry horses had to carry a considerable burden. Large horses were required, and this meant that they were relatively slow, and found it difficult to change pace or direction quickly.

Infantry

At the start of the Crusades, the ordinary foot-soldier was considered inferior in every respect to the knight on horseback.

Foot-soldiers were equipped in a very haphazard fashion. Some, for example, were armed only with daggers. Body protection was also irregular. A few soldiers wore head armour, but these were the fortunate few. Most of them, however, did have a jacket of thick leather or quilted cloth which, although useless against swords and lances, offered some protection against arrows. The chroniclers often described Crusader infantrymen wearing these jackets as pin cushions. The Saracen Beha-ed-Din, for example, wrote: "I saw some (Crusaders) with ten arrows fixed in their backs, yet marching along at their ordinary pace."

A small number of foot-soldiers were armed with the shortbow. But, as the Crusade era continued, the shortbow was superseded by the vastly superior crossbow, which fired metal bolts or arrows farther, faster and generally more accurately than any of the earlier bows. Another infantry weapon which was

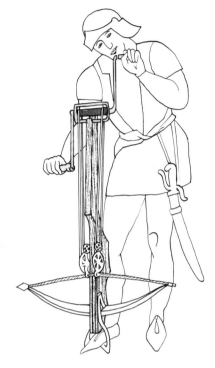

As their weapons developed, archers played an increasingly important part in the Crusades (*below*).
Above A crossbowman winds his weapon. But this was a slow, clumsy process, and the longbow (*right*) proved more effective in war.

becoming increasingly common was the halberd. This was a pike which had an axehead near the point, to allow the weapon to be used for cutting as well as thrusting.

In addition, towards the end of the Crusades, the English longbow was introduced. The longbow was originally a Welsh weapon, and was discovered by Edward I during his conquest of Wales. It had twice the range of the crossbow, and could be fired rapidly and with great accuracy by the skilled English archers.

Increasingly, as these efficient weapons were introduced, and the heavily-armoured knights became less and less mobile, the infantry acquired a new role, a new status. Meanwhile, at the start of the Crusades, the foot-soldiers merely tagged along behind the arrogant knights. Rolf saw them being bullied and pushed about as if they were cattle. They had the minimum of training, they could expect little in the way of bodily confort, and soon they would come face to face with the vicious and brutal Saracen warriors.

The Saracens

Horsemen also formed the most important part of the Saracen armies, which sometimes used no foot-soldiers at all. But, unlike the Crusader knights, the Saracen cavalry fired arrows from horseback, often with deadly effect.

The Crusaders did experiment for a time with mounted crossbowmen, but they found that the increased strength of the horsemen was cancelled out by the decreased accuracy and slower rate of fire of the crossbows. The Saracens, on the other hand, used light bows, and depended upon sheer volume of fire rather than accuracy. Mounted on lighter and faster horses than the Crusaders, the Saracen horsemen would gallop to within range, unleash a massive swarm of arrows, and then wheel aside to allow a second wave to fire.

For close combat, the Saracens used short, light, and razor-sharp curved scimitars. These were made from finest steel according to some secret formula, and were amazingly flexible yet strong.

One Crusader wrote: "The Turks were not loaded with armour like our men, and their ease of movement was very disconcerting to us. For the most part they were lightly armed, carrying only a bow, or a mace bristling with sharp teeth, a scimitar, a light spear with an iron head, and a dagger. When put to flight by a greater force, they fled away on horseback with the utmost rapidity. Their agility is unequalled throughout the world. If they see their pursuers stop, they will usually turn round and come back – like the fly which, if you drive it away, will go, but the minute it sees you stop will return."

The Crusade to which Rolf belonged, the First, was fortunate in one important respect – it did not

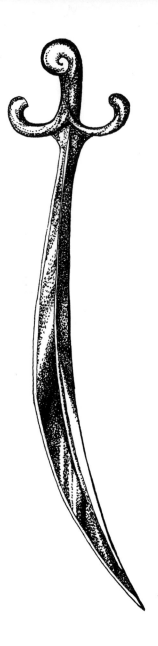

Above The Saracen warrior fought with the short, light, and razor-sharp scimitar. This was a deadly weapon in close combat.

come up against the greatest of all the Saracen leaders, the dreaded Saladin.

This Moslem Sultan, born in Kurdish territory which is part of modern Iraq, reigned for twenty-four years, and plagued most of the later Crusades. He displayed a high degree of military courage, and developed methods of using his flexible horsemen to divide the opposing army into small groups, after which each group was attacked and defeated in turn.

Above Saladin, who led the Saracen forces during the later Crusades, was a great military commander and a formidable enemy.
Right The Saracens were lightly-armed and relied on speed to win the advantage.

The Mongols

Mongol hordes under Genghis Khan came thrusting from their harsh territory north of China in 1220, in one of the most violent and explosive invasions the world has ever known. The Great Khan and his successors carved a gigantic empire, hacked out of the Middle and Near East by cruelty, barbarism and brilliant skill.

These Mongols, like the Saracen Turks (many of whom were themselves descended from Mongol tribes), relied for success upon fast-moving horsemen, carefully organized and superbly trained.

About forty per cent of a Mongol army consisted of heavy cavalry. These men, who wore head-to-toe armour and rode heavy horses, provided the shock units. The rest of the army were light cavalry, wearing no armour at all apart from helmets, but carrying long-range bows, javelins and lassoes. Each man had with him two quivers of arrows, and one or more spare horses which were herded along behind the columns.

All Mongol cavalrymen would put on shirts of strong raw silk just before battle. Arrows could not penetrate this silk, but instead pushed the cloth into the wound intact. Chinese surgeons, travelling with the army, were then able to pull out the arrow heads by tugging on the silk.

The Mongols were the best-trained soldiers of their time, and brilliant horsemen. Units worked closely with each other, and each troop, squadron, and regiment was capable of precise manoeuvres. Attacks were always rapid and daring. The enemy was usually thrown off balance by the lightning offensive policy, and was rarely able to recover.

QUIVER
BOWCASE

44

One result of the Mongols' skill was the exaggerated view of the number of men in these "hordes." In fact, the Mongol army was usually very much smaller than that of the enemy. The force of two hundred and forty thousand men which swooped westwards under Genghis Khan was the largest that the Mongols ever put into the field.

Above During the thirteenth century, the fierce Mongols, under the leadership of Genghis Khan, threatened Europe and the Holy Land with their brutality and barbarism. Their armies consisted mainly of horsemen, but only the members of the heavy cavalry (*right*) wore armour. The light cavalry (*left*) relied on speed and superb horsemanship for their protection.

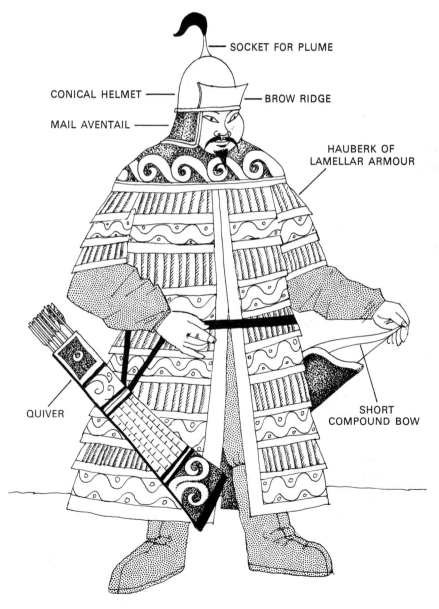

SOCKET FOR PLUME

CONICAL HELMET

BROW RIDGE

MAIL AVENTAIL

HAUBERK OF LAMELLAR ARMOUR

QUIVER

SHORT COMPOUND BOW

3. War

Christians, Turks, Arabs and Mongols were all participants in the mighty struggle which was to stretch over two centuries. Christians from the woods and forests of England and France, from the flat lowlands of Belgium, from the cold Scandinavian mountains, from the hot Spanish hills and from the deep, dark Rhine valley; savage Turks and Arabs from the dusty deserts of the Middle East and the North African shores; and mighty Mongols from the barren steppes of Central Asia.

Kings, princes, bishops, sultans, knights, infantrymen, and ordinary humble peasants like Rolf were all thrown into this whirlpool. East and West met in terrible combat, tearing one another to shreds as they fought for the ancient relics of Christianity in the Holy Land. Territory was won, and lost, and won again. Infidel and Christian skeletons were heaped together in the sand, and bleached by the same scorching sun.

Four main Crusades were launched. And the influence of these expeditions rippled far back to the forests and mountains in the north whence they came, and to the distant Asian wastes. Whole nations and entire generations were affected by the struggle.

But now we travel with Rolf, and the other soldiers and civilians, as they make their dangerous way across Europe to take part in this grim and brutal war.

Right Crusaders and Moslems hack ruthlessly at each other as they meet in ferocious and bloody combat in the Holy Land.

Onward Christian soldiers

More and more men join the Crusade as the throng shuffles down through France towards Constantinople. Rolf sees husbands bidding farewell to their wives, and children to their parents, as he walks through towns and villages.

"Oh, the groans of those who embraced at parting!" wrote one Crusader. "The good wishes for those who were going away! Oh, the eyes heavy with tears, sobs interrupting the speakers amid the kisses of those who were dear to them."

Rolf and his comrades in the First Crusade are taking the land route to Constantinople. When they reach Cologne, they split into two main columns. Rolf and his master cross east to the upper reaches of the Danube, and follow the mighty river down, via Vienna, Budapest and Belgrade. Then, they cut southwards through modern Yugoslavia to Adrianople and thence to Constantinople. Meanwhile the second column is taking a more southerly route to Geneva, Milan, Trieste and from there to Greece, and Constantinople.

Rolf's impression of the chaos surrounding the

Above right The routes taken by the members of the First Crusade. The journey was long and hazardous, and travelling in the small, cramped ships (*below*) was as arduous and exhausting as following the route overland.

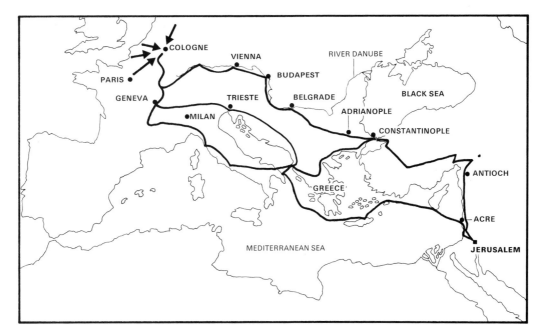

First Crusade is constantly being strengthened. Great lords have brought their wives and families, and each lady has her serving women, cooks, musicians, scribes and pages. Every lord has his servants. Behind them come a vast horde of camp followers – priests, old men and women, children, and tradespeople. Rolf sees an increasing number slumped in the ditches by the roadside, faint or even dead from exhaustion.

"It is a marvellous and most laughable sight," wrote one cynical eye-witness. "Troops of poor folk bearing their few possessions in their two-wheeled carts, while their children, as soon as they come to some walled town, ask again and again if this is Jerusalem."

Travel was no less arduous when Richard I took the sea route with his Third Crusade. "The roar of the dashing waves, and the ships creaking with the violence of the wind," wrote one member of the court, "struck all with no small terror . . . All management of the ships was at an end as they were borne hither and thither on the waves . . ."

The Holy Land

Rolf and the rest of his group stagger exhausted into Constantinople after their long journey across Europe. And for weeks after their arrival, stragglers continue to reach this temporary refuge in small, weary parties.

The kings and great generals always try to summon a show of splendour for their arrival in the capital of eastern Christendom. Even Rolf's lord tells him to repair the tattered clothing, to polish

Above The city of Constantinople was a source of wonder to the exhausted Crusaders – but it was only a temporary refuge.

50

the tarnished weapons, and to groom his horses till they shine like satin.

An eyewitness later described the scene when Richard I reached Messina, the capital of Sicily, on his way to Palestine. "When report was spread of the coming of the noble King of England, the people of Messina rushed eagerly to catch a glimpse of him. And lo! they beheld the sea in the distance covered with galleys; and the sound of trumpets, loud and shrill struck upon the ear!

"The galleys were laden and adorned with arms of all kinds, their pennons and standards floating in countless numbers upon the breeze. The prows of the galleys were distinguished from one another by bright and varied colours; their shields glittered in the sun, and the sea boiled under their oars.

"Then lo! the magnificent King stands on a prow more elevated and ornamented than the rest, and lands in splendid dress. The sailors sent before him bring forward the horses, that he and his suite might mount and ride away."

Rolf wanders wide-eyed through Constantinople, and stuffs himself with strange exotic foods – pomegranates, oranges, figs and watermelons. Yet, despite this sanctuary, stern tasks lie ahead. The worst part of the journey has still to be attempted.

Rolf and the others in the First Crusade must cross the narrow straits of the Bosphorus, which lie between the Black Sea and the Aegean. Then they must advance through Turkish territory, via Nicaea, and across the vast salt deserts of central Asia Minor.

Such hardship wrought a ruthless weeding-out process. Only the fittest survived. The army now became professional, as hard and unrelenting as the deserts with which it was forced to contend.

Life on the road

Even without large scale battles, Rolf found everyday life on the road extremely harsh. The enemy practised a form of conflict known later as guerrilla warfare, and Saracens were always ready to pounce upon the unwary.

One Crusader wrote: "The Saracens came every night into our camp on foot, and killed our men where they found them sleeping. In this way, they killed my Lord of Courtenay's sentinel. They cut off his head and took it away with them, and left his body lying on a table."

Diseases swept through the troops. This same Crusader described the situation when his army camped near a river clogged with bodies from a recent battle. "The only fish we had to eat in camp for the whole of Lent were eels which, being greedy creatures, feed on the dead. On account of this evil circumstance, and because of the unhealthy climate . . . a disease spread through the army, of such a sort that the flesh on our legs dried up, and the skin became covered with black spots. No one who fell a

Below The land the Crusaders had to cross was harsh and barren and the men suffered from starvation and disease. But medical practices were still crude (*right*) and few of those who fell ill could hope to recover.

victim to this disease could hope to recover."

Food was usually scarce while forces were out on campaign, for the surrounding wasteland could not supply enough for such a multitude of men. The Mongols solved this problem in a way which sickened even the hardened Christians. "The soldiers put uncooked meat between their saddles and the tails of their coats," reported one English eyewitness, "and when the blood is well pressed out they eat it quite raw. What they cannot eat at the moment they throw into a leather bag. I myself once saw a Mongol open his bag, and as he did so we held our noses, unable to bear the horrible stench."

Night brought no real rest from the daily toil. "As each night came round," wrote another Crusader, "a sort of reptile attacked us, commonly called *tarrentes*, which crept on the ground and had most venomous stings. Those they stung were instantly swelled with the venom and tortured with pains."

Guerrilla attacks, disease, shortage of food, and attacks by tarantulas and scorpions – all these had to be endured, as well as the perils of battle.

Battle tactics

Tactics, or methods of fighting battles, changed considerably during the Crusades, mainly as a result of the experiences gained; and these alterations give the Crusades an important place in the history of warfare.

Rolf experienced the earlier methods of fighting when forces from the First Crusade clashed with the Turks on their way south from Constantinople. The enemy Saracens appeared on the skyline. The

Below The cumbersome Crusader knights rode slow heavy horses. This meant they were an easy prey for their flexible and more mobile enemy.

Christian column halted, still an apparently chaotic mass, though with the knights clustered together to one side. Infantrymen gathered in a jumbled crowd, while the servants – Rolf among them – ran back to a low hill to be out of the way.

Rolf saw the knights form into a rough line. Then, as the Turks galloped down towards the Crusader army, they began their charge. It was a terrifying sight – the two lines of horsemen met in a gigantic clash. Rolf could see swords and axes being raised and slashed downwards. Turks and Crusaders were locked together. But the latter, because of their added weight and armour, forced the enemy to retreat. Some knights plunged on in pursuit, while the rest pulled to one side and attempted to reorganize themselves.

Only at this stage did the Crusader infantry join in the battle. They ran forward to slaughter the enemy cavalrymen who had been thrown from their horses by the knights, and fired their arrows after the retreating enemy.

But the Saracens soon saw the advantages of being more flexible than the cumbersome Crusader knights. They used fast ponies, darting to right and left to avoid the slower knights, and firing their arrows behind them.

In an attempt to protect the Crusader knights against this greater enemy mobility, the infantry were gradually brought into play. Foot soldiers began to provide a shield for the knights, and archery was developed. By the end of the twelfth century, instead of knights doing most of the fighting, battles more often began with tremendous crossbow volleys. Only then would the knights emerge from behind the infantry base to charge down upon the enemy.

Eyewitness account

Above Richard the Lionheart and Saladin meet face to face as Crusaders and Saracens clash in ferocious combat.

Some Crusaders left vivid reports of the battles in which they participated. One such eyewitness account was written by an anonymous soldier in Richard I's army, who had taken part in the massive clash with Saladin's forces at Arsuf, on 7th September, 1191. His description illustrates the differences between later tactics and those witnessed by Rolf.

Richard was pressing towards Jerusalem when Saladin's army sprang at them from a prepared

ambush. "It was nearly nine o'clock when there appeared a large body of Turks, ten thousand strong, coming down upon us at full charge, throwing darts and arrows as fast as they could, while their voices mingled in one terrible yell . . .

"Following after them came an infernal race of men, black as hell in colour . . . With them also were the Saracens who live in the desert, called Bedouins – they are a savage race of men, blacker than soot, who fight on foot.

"Beyond them I could see the well-arranged phalanxes of the Turks, with ensigns fixed to their lances, and standard and banners easily distinguished . . . In an irresistible charge, their horses swifter than eagles and urged on like lightning, they attacked our men; and the whole sky was darkened . . .

"Oh, how obstinately they pressed and continued their stubborn attacks, so that our men lost many horses, killed by their darts and arrows! Oh, how useful to us on that day were our bowmen, who closed the extremities of the lines and did their best to repel the obstinate Turks!

"The enemy thundered at their backs as if with mallets, so that having no room to use their bows, they fought hand to hand with swords, lances and clubs; and the blows of the Turks, echoing from their metal armour, resounded as if they had been struck upon an anvil."

Richard's infantry were forming a protective screen for the knights. And the King had given orders for a counter-attack to be launched as soon as his men received a pre-arranged signal. This command Richard would give when he believed the enemy were sufficiently disorganized after their charge, and the clash with his infantry. Then, and only then, would the Crusader knights pound forward.

Carnage

"It had been resolved," reported the anonymous chronicler at Arsuf, "that the sounding of six trumpets in three different parts of the army should be the signal for the charge."

And now the six trumpets shrilled the command. "Those who were in the first line made a united and furious charge; after them the men of Poitou, the Bretons, and the men of Anjou, rushed swiftly onward, and then came the rest of the army in a body: each troop showed its valour and boldly closed with the Turks, transfixing them with their lances and casting them to the ground.

"The sky grew black with the dust which was raised in the confusion of that encounter. The Turks, who had purposely dismounted from their horses in order to take better aim at our men with their darts and arrows, were slain on all sides in that charge. Having been thrown over by our cavalry, the Turks were beheaded by our foot-soldiers.

"King Richard, seeing his army move forward, spurred his horse on at full speed and broke into the ranks of the Turkish infantry . . . Then were men thrown to the ground, the wounded lamenting with groans their hard fate, others drawing their last breath weltering in gore. And many lay headless while their lifeless forms were trodden under foot alike by friend and foe."

Dead Turks were spread over half a mile of bloodstained earth. "The rest of the enemy were repulsed in so wonderful a manner that for the space of two miles nothing could be seen but fugitives."

About seven thousand of Saladin's men were slain at Arsuf, while Richard lost only about seven hundred. This disproportion between loser and

victor was common, for knights, especially those wearing heavy armour, were helpless once their ranks had been disrupted. They were easy victims for the foot-soldiers with their pikes, axes and swords.

Carnage in battle was often appalling. This same writer described another occasion when the Crusaders had thrown the enemy into confusion, and advanced to reap the benefit. "Swords flashed in the air and the ground was covered with blood. Bodies were torn limb from limb; heads, arms, feet and hands, and other fragments lay scattered about."

Left Once the heavily armoured knights had been unhorsed, they made easy victims for the more agile foot-soldiers.

Siege

Christian and Moslem armies met not only in pitched battles – they also frequently clashed in long and violent sieges. These too resulted in awesome slaughter.

It was during sieges that the Crusaders were first confronted with "Greek fire," an explosive mixture of asphalt and crude petroleum. This liquid fire was projected from siphons over the besieging troops as they attempted to clamber up the city walls, or was poured into glass containers which were thrown like hand-grenades, bursting on impact to ignite the contents.

Another missile used in siege warfare was a clay jar crammed with poisonous snakes. And boiling tar was often poured onto assailants.

Massive siege machines were constructed during the Crusades. These included the *beffroi*, or siege tower, a tall wooden tower on wheels which was dragged up to the walls. At the top of this tower was a drawbridge which, when let down onto the wall, allowed the men inside to run across and grapple with the city's defenders.

Below A common siege machine was the mangonel, which worked like an enormous catapult.

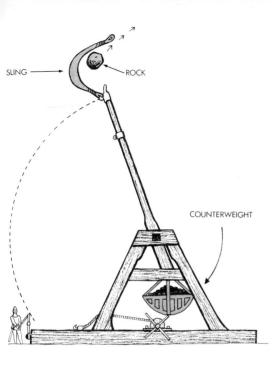

SLING → ROCK

COUNTERWEIGHT

Left The trebuchet was often used to fling huge stones over the city walls.

Below The Crusaders had no proper supply lines and usually suffered as much as the cities they were besieging.

Other machines, including the mangonel and the trebuchet, could fling huge stones over the walls, rather like enormous catapults. One stone could kill as many as ten men.

Rolf took part in perhaps the most famous of all Crusader sieges – the siege of Antioch. It began on 21st October, 1097, and lasted for seven terrible months. Both sides suffered appalling losses. The Crusaders camped outside the city walls and Rolf ate lizards and snakes in an attempt to satisfy his gnawing hunger. His lips were black and cracked from the heat and from thirst.

The siege ended when one of the Crusaders' leaders, Bohemond, struck a bargain with a traitorous Turkish emir. The Christian army moved in, and Rolf watched in horror the terrible massacre which ensued. Few Turks escaped with their lives, although some strong Saracens managed to fight their way back to the inner citadel of the city.

Then, only three days later, Rolf and the other Crusaders received terrible news. A Turkish army, two hundred thousand men strong, was approaching the city. Within hours, the victorious Crusaders were in turn themselves besieged.

61

Antioch agony

Conditions inside Antioch deteriorated rapidly. Trapped within the battered walls by the Turkish reinforcements under the command of Kerboga, and with the Turks in the inner citadel still controlling the water supply, the Crusaders suffered increasing agony. Rolf sat huddled in a corner, his eyes closed, his mind dazed by the sun and the lack of food.

No help came from Constantinople, and the siege continued for over a month. Then a miracle occurred inside the besieged city. A humble priest, Peter Bartholomew, claimed that St. Andrew had appeared before him, and had told him that the actual spear which had pierced Christ's side as he hung on the cross was now buried in Antioch.

Rolf summoned his remaining strength to join the soldiers who were digging for this holy relic beneath the Church of St. Peter. And he was with the desperate Christians when an old lance-head was unearthed. He shouted and cheered with the rest. A tremendous religious fervour inflamed the soldiers, and they sallied forth to attack the besieging Turks. The ragged Crusader troops thrust forward as if drunk -- slashing, clubbing and tearing at the Turks with their bare hands. The enemy were astonished and dismayed by this transformation. They broke ranks before the fierce, hysterical onslaught, and started to flee. Crusaders followed, hacking and hewing at the Saracens with their swords and spears. The result was a tremendous victory.

Yet, despite this success, more and more of the Crusaders began to doubt whether the Holy Lance was genuine. Feeling started to rise against the

Right The city of Antioch, where the Crusaders were trapped between two Turkish forces.
Below The weary and desperate Crusaders kneel in thanksgiving prayer as the Holy Lance is discovered beneath the Church of St. Peter in Antioch.

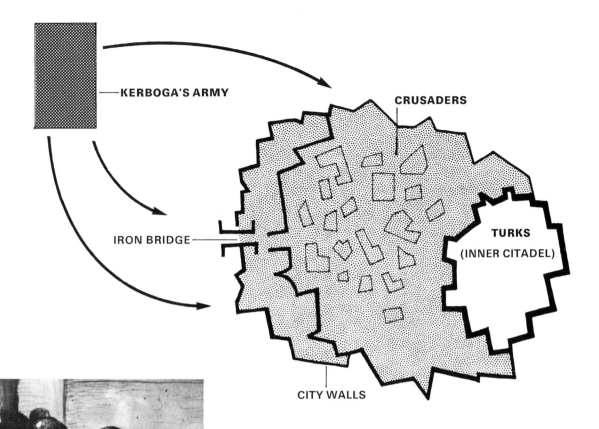

KERBOGA'S ARMY

CRUSADERS

IRON BRIDGE

TURKS
(INNER CITADEL)

CITY WALLS

unfortunate Peter Bartholomew, and the Crusaders decided to put him to the test. Two huge bonfires were lit, and the scorching ashes were then spread over a wide area. The priest was dragged forward, and forced to walk barefoot across the glowing embers. If he managed to do so, unharmed, then he would be judged not guilty of fraud.

Rolf saw Peter accomplish this feat, not just once, but twice. He joined in the massive cheers. And he watched the humble priest standing, smiling, as men surged forward to congratulate him, and to touch this apparent saint. And Rolf saw Peter trampled to death in the crush.

After Antioch, the First Crusade moved on to lay siege to Jerusalem. Complete victory now seemed within their grasp.

63

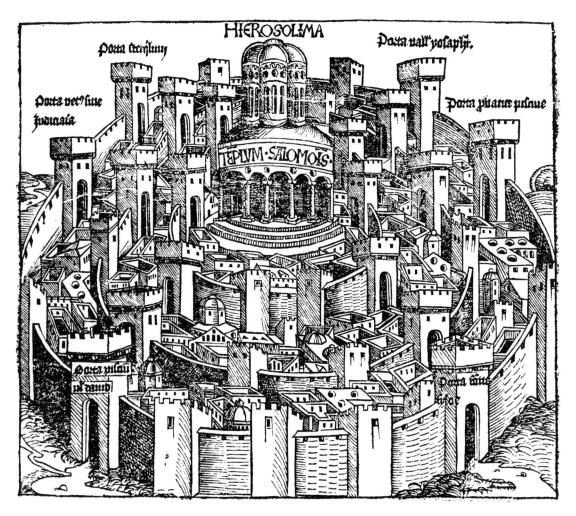

Labels on image:
HIEROSOLIMA
Porta Ephraim
Porta vallis Iosaphat
Porta veteris sive Iudiciaria
Porta pratie piscine
TEMPLUM SALOMONIS
Porta pilati vel david
Porta montis Syon

Occupation

After the capture of Jerusalem in the summer of 1099, a long period of quieter activity begins.

Some Christians spread out to establish themselves in other important areas, which become known as the Crusader States. These include Jerusalem, Edessa, Antioch, and Tripoli. Rolf, however, stays in Jerusalem with his master. And life is now an unbelievable dream compared with the existence he

Although the Crusaders succeeded in capturing Jerusalem (*above* and *top right*), life was still precarious and Moslem raids and resistance continued.

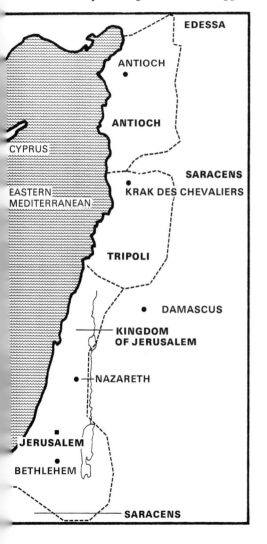

Below The Crusader States set up in the Holy Land after the capture of Jerusalem in 1099.

EDESSA

ANTIOCH

ANTIOCH

CYPRUS

SARACENS
KRAK DES CHEVALIERS

EASTERN
MEDITERRANEAN

TRIPOLI

DAMASCUS

KINGDOM
OF JERUSALEM

NAZARETH

JERUSALEM

BETHLEHEM

SARACENS

had known at home.

Instead of the dark, dank hovel, he lives with his lord in a bright, sunlit house. Elaborate paintings adorn the ceilings. The floors are covered with carpets or delicate mosaic-patterned tiles. The rooms are filled with elegant furniture. Rolf's lord wears a smooth silk robe. Women, although always veiled in the streets, cover their faces with exciting cosmetics. Spiced foods and exotic sweets tempt Rolf's ready appetite. His lord lives in richer surroundings than many a prince back home in Europe.

And yet, despite the luxuries, danger remains constant. Pitched battles are infrequent, but skirmishing continues. Although the Crusaders attempt to strengthen their positions and to extend the four main areas of occupation, progress remains slow. Isolated areas even within the four Crusader states, remain under Moslem control. Moslem raids from the inland territory continued. And the Crusaders are unable to sever the Moslem communication link between Syria and Egypt.

Moreover, even in the heart of the Crusader States, life is still precarious. Rolf's lord does not allow a Moslem servant to pour his wine, for fear some vile poison might be slipped into the glass. Dead Crusaders are found in the streets, with daggers thrust between their shoulders. Tension underlies the apparent easy life.

Indeed, this period of occupation sees the growth of a new type of fighter, known as the "Assassin." It also witnesses the rise of two new orders of Christian soldiers, whose names would soon strike fear in Saracen hearts – the Hospitallers and the Templars.

Assassins and Knights

Hasan as-Sabath, a Persian who lived in the last half of the eleventh century, created the violent Moslem sect known as the Hashishiyum – the Assassins. These fanatics fought primarily against the Seljuk Turks, and the Arab rulers in Baghdad, the Abbasid.

The Assassins, therefore, shared a common enemy with the Crusaders, and Christian-Assassin alliances were frequently attempted. But the Crusaders never entirely trusted these skilled and cruel murderers, and with good reason. Their stealth, their secret organization, and the widespread support which they enjoyed made them vicious enemies and doubtful friends.

Rolf and his master left Jerusalem and began their long journey home in 1101. The year before, the Crusaders had themselves founded a new military organization, which was already becoming increasingly powerful.

This order, known as the Knights of St. John and later as the Hospitallers, was originally intended to take care of poor pilgrims who travelled to Jerusalem. But soon its members became an influential and largely independent military force, owing allegiance to no one but the Pope.

In 1123, an even more powerful order was created. This was the Knights Templar, which soon became feared throughout the Holy Land. The Templars were well-organized and disciplined, and were distinguished by their white tunics marked with big red crosses.

The fame of the Templars spread throughout Europe. Young nobles flocked to join the Order, and men donated huge sums of money to finance

66

the movement. This income allowed the Templars a great deal of independence. Like the Hospitallers, they were able to stand apart from the petty quarrels and rivalry between the various Christian leaders in the Holy Land.

The Hospitallers and Templars provided an element of stability in the Holy Land – while many Crusaders, like Rolf's lord, came and went, they remained. As a result of their strength and experience they undertook all the most difficult tasks. However, because of their military power and wealth, the Templars were increasingly disliked and feared by their fellow Christians. And later, after the decline of the Crusades, they suffered persecution, torture and death.

Above The badge of the Knights of St. John can still be seen today – it is the badge of the St. John's Ambulance Brigade.

Left The Knights Templar at work in Jerusalem. Notice their distinctive tunics marked with a large red cross.

67

4. The different Crusades

From the year 1096 onwards, a constant stream of warriors, pilgrims and ordinary citizens flowed to and from the Holy Land. They left their homes full of hopes of adventure, riches and religious fulfilment. Those who returned, like Rolf, had exciting tales to tell. Anecdotes of adventures became almost commonplace. Riches were also brought home, especially the proceeds of plunder.

One Crusader gave this description of the captured contents of a Saracen camel train. "They brought mules loaded with spices of different kinds, and of great value; gold and silver; cloaks of silk; purple and scarlet robes, and various ornamented apparel; besides arms and weapons of divers forms; coats of mail; costly cushions, pavilions, tents, biscuits, bread . . . a large quantity of conserves and medicines; basins and chessboards; silver dishes and candlesticks . . ."

Such tales encouraged others to trek to the East. The title "Crusade" spread far afield, and was applied to many small and insignificant expeditions. In all four major Crusades were launched, as well as four of a smaller size.

Rolf's experiences revealed some aspects of the First Crusade. But he knew nothing of its planning nor of its aims. And the fighting which he saw represented only a minor portion of this great expedition. There was very much more to the Crusades than met the individual eye.

Right Soldiers returning from the Crusades brought with them many riches and works of art, and told tales of the great wealth to be found in the East.

Friction

Pope Urban's appeal led, in the first place, to the disastrous People's Crusade. While this foolish expedition was meeting its doom in 1096, warriors of the official First Crusade were making their various ways to Constantinople, which had been selected as the Crusaders' rallying point.

The Byzantine Emperor, Alexius, was astounded by the force which converged on his city. When he had appealed to Pope Urban for help, he had been

Above The soldiers of the First Crusade took part in many sieges, which were often followed by awesome slaughter and plunder.

seeking a few professional soldiers to strengthen his own armies against the Turks, not this vast unruly horde.

Long-standing religious and political differences between the Byzantines and the Western Europeans made the Emperor immediately suspicious of Crusader intentions. Alexius was especially worried by the presence among the Crusade leaders of Bohemond, son of the Norman commander Robert Guiscard, who had expelled Byzantine forces from southern Italy in 1082. Relations were sour from the start. Moreover, Alexius had no real interest in rescuing Jerusàlem. He only wanted to see his former possessions in Asia Minor restored.

But, by the spring of 1097, some kind of bargain had been struck. In exchange for help from Alexius, the Crusaders promised to assist in the recapture of Nicaea, and to return any other former Byzantine possessions which they might wrest from the Turks.

On 14th May, 1097, siege was laid to Nicaea. The city surrendered on 19th June. Alexius had carefully arranged for this surrender to be made to him, rather than to the Crusaders, whom he still distrusted.

After Nicaea, the army split into two columns. The left-hand section was led by the harsh and sinister Bohemond, whose short-clipped yellow hair and beardless face caused amazement among the Byzantines. They regarded a beard as a necessary sign of manhood.

On July 1st, 1097, Bohemond had the chance to prove his manliness. Massive Turkish cavalry units suddenly appeared, and moments later they began swooping in for the attack, screaming and flourishing their terrible scimitars.

On to Jerusalem

Crusader knights rode out to clash with the advancing Turks in a melee of whinnying horses, ringing swords, shrieking men, and swirling, choking dust. Footsoldiers hurried to build crude fortifications.

Repeated Crusader charges failed to halt the enemy, and the Turks appeared ready to slice directly through the centre of the hard-pressed Christian column. But Bohemond sent riders to force their way through the surrounding enemy, and gallop their foaming horses across country to fetch help from the other Crusader force.

Just in time, heavy cavalry from this second host, led by Godfrey de Bouillon and Raymond, Count of Toulouse, crashed into the Turks from the rear. Caught in a vice, the Turks were ruthlessly slaughtered. Survivors fled, leaving three thousand dead. But the Crusaders had lost almost four thousand men.

The Christians resumed their difficult advance and fought their way on to Antioch. There the siege witnessed by Rolf was followed by the miraculous affair of the Holy Lance. After this Crusader triumph, and the bickering which ensued, the Crusaders moved on towards Jerusalem, leaving Bohemond with a secondary force in charge at Antioch.

The Crusaders advanced slowly down the coast to Jaffa, where they turned inland towards the Holy City. On 7th June, 1099, the siege of Jerusalem began.

The attackers suffered terribly from lack of food and water. "We were so grieved with thirst," wrote one participant, "that we sewed hides of oxen and buffaloes, wherein we brought water from a distance

Right The Crusaders used a massive wooden tower to cross the walls of Jerusalem when they besieged the town in 1099. They rampaged through the streets and slaughtered the Turks mercilessly, killing even those who had sought refuge in the churches and mosques (*above*).

of some six miles. From these vessels we sucked
stinking liquid."

The Crusaders built a massive wooden siege
tower and a battering ram, and pushed forward
against the city walls. Godfrey was almost demented
on hearing that his rival, Raymond of Toulouse,
might enter the city first, and led the way shouting
and raging onto the Turkish battlements.

By 18th July, the city had fallen. Crusaders rampaged through the streets, massacring Saracens and
civilians. And the First Crusade had accomplished
its purpose.

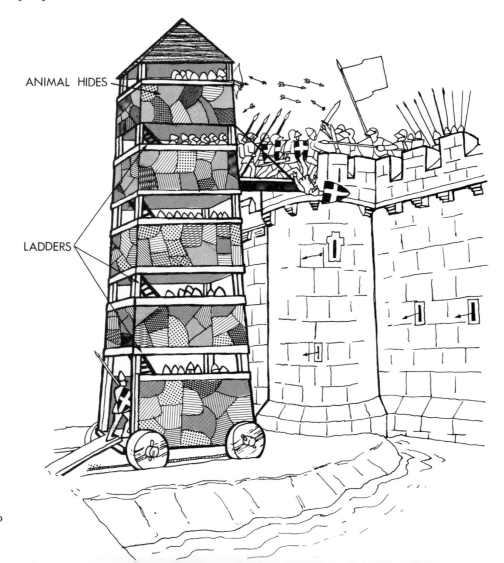

ANIMAL HIDES

LADDERS

D

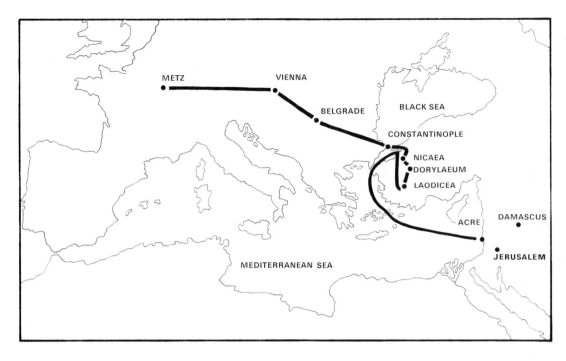

The Second Crusade

Above left The route taken by the soldiers of the ill-fated Second Crusade.

Eight days after the capture of Jerusalem, Godfrey de Bouillon walked barefoot in a plain linen shift to worship at the Holy Sepulchre. The victorious Crusaders had elected him Prince of the city. But Godfrey, for fear of antagonizing the Christian monarchs in Europe, refused to take the actual title of King.

Less than a year later, however, Godfrey died, and his brother Baldwin took control. Baldwin was much less scrupulous, and immediately proclaimed himself King of Jerusalem. The other three Crusader States -- Edessa, Antioch and Tripoli -- were officially made subject to his authority, although in practice they remained independent.

This was the beginning of a long period of occupation, dominated by skirmishes with the still

Above The Crusaders fight desperately as Saladin's forces lay siege to Jerusalem.

Left Louis VII of France is blessed by men of the Church as he sets out for the Holy Land.

powerful Moslems. In 1144, they succeeded in capturing Edessa, and this disaster prompted a papal call for another Crusade. An ill-fated expedition set out in 1147. Its principal leaders were Emperor Conrad III of Germany and King Louis VII of France. The main German and French armies took different routes south from Constantinople. The German army, under Conrad, ran out of food near Dorylaeum, and the starving Crusaders were overwhelmed by a Turkish attack. Conrad and a few survivors managed to stagger back to Nicaea, whence they sailed to Palestine.

The French, led by King Louis, had taken a longer route, but this failed to save them from the marauding Moslems. After an indecisive battle east of Laodicea, Louis embarked his cavalry and went by sea to Palestine, leaving his infantry to continue alone. Most of them were massacred by the Turks.

In 1148, the two disillusioned rulers, Conrad and Louis, joined King Baldwin III of Jerusalem in an expedition against Damascus. But although they managed to take the city, the three leaders were soon arguing and bickering amongst themselves, and eventually parted company again.

In June, 1187, the great Moslem leader, Saladin, invaded Palestine. On 4th July, he defeated the Crusaders under Guy of Jerusalem at the Battle of Hattin, and then moved on to capture the Holy City itself. By 1192, it was clearly urgent to organize another Crusade. Among those who answered the Pope's call was King Richard I of England, the Lionheart.

The Third Crusade

The Third Crusade moved in two main sections. In 1189, Frederick I of Germany led thirty thousand men overland to Constantinople. The following year, Richard the Lionheart and Philip II of France sailed with their forces across the Mediterranean.

Frederick's men advanced south against the Turks, but the German Emperor was drowned. His son took over command, but he lacked his father's ability, and many of his men died from starvation and disease.

Meanwhile Richard and Philip reached Sicily, where they spent the winter of 1190–91 in constant quarrelling. The following spring, Philip sailed for Acre, while Richard delayed to conquer Cyprus for use as a base.

Richard arrived at Acre on 8th June. The city had been besieged by the Christians for the past two years, but at last the Crusaders drove off Saladin's army, and forced the inhabitants to surrender. The French King then returned home, leaving Richard as sole commander. The English King proceeded to show his considerable military skill, and brutality. His cruelty was such that, for many years, Saracen women frightened their children by threatening that Richard would deal with them if they did not behave.

In the summer of 1191, Richard began his march towards Jerusalem. He kept near the coast, and carefully avoided dispersing his forces. This way, he hoped to prevent Saladin from repeating the tactics he had used so successfully at Hattin in 1187.

But the Moslem leader still displayed his cunning. Saladin withdrew before Richard, practising a "scorched earth" policy. He destroyed all the crops,

Above Richard the Lionheart watches the execution of Saracen hostages after the siege of Acre in 1191.
Opposite The route taken by Richard I to the Holy Land.

and poisoned all the wells along the way. Lack of water, food and fodder, and constant arguments, made Richard lose all enthusiasm for the long campaign.

Negotiations between the Saracens and Christians started, broke off, and started again. Richard had proved himself an excellent military leader, but he failed sadly as a negotiator. Finally on 2nd September, 1192, a treaty with Saladin was settled. All coastal cities as far south as Jaffa remained in Christian control. The Saracens, however, continued to occupy the Holy City, Jerusalem, although pilgrims were now allowed to visit the sacred places.

The Kingdom of Jerusalem was thus deprived of its capital. And, as Richard's ships disappeared over the horizon, Crusader territory was reduced to a mere coastal strip about ten miles wide and ninety miles long.

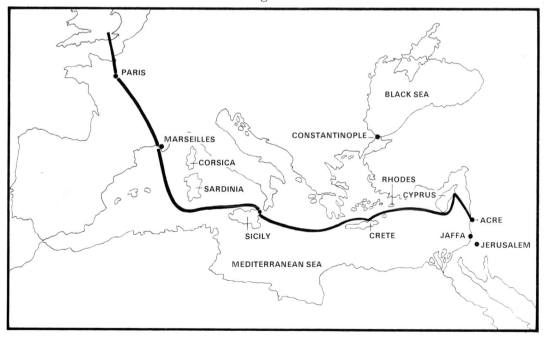

Later Crusades

All heart had now gone from the Crusades. Pope
Innocent III, elected in 1198, did call for another
effort – but this one, begun in 1200, was aimed as
much against the Byzantine Empire based on
Constantinople as against the Saracens.

The Fourth Crusade, however, never reached
the Holy Land. Instead, after months of fighting
against the Byzantines, the Crusaders took Constantinople in April, 1204. They immediately wal-
lowed in an orgy of sacking, plunder and massacre.

In 1215, Innocent III launched yet another
Crusade, and this, the Fifth, was decisively repulsed
by Moslems under Malik al-Kamil. The Sixth
Crusade, led by Frederick II of Germany, was
launched in 1228. Frederick, more through di-
plomacy than military means, succeeded in taking
over Jerusalem, Nazareth, and Bethlehem, together
with a land corridor to the coast.

But now came a new and even more terrible
threat, from the Mongols in the East. These fierce
warriors clashed against the old Crusader enemies,
the Seljuk Turks, and established control over
Anatolia in 1243. Meanwhile the Seventh Crusade,
launched in reaction to the Moslem capture of
Jerusalem and led by King Louis IX of France, was
decisively defeated by the Egyptian Moslems in
1250.

The Crusaders found themselves wedged in
between the Egyptians and the Mongols. These two
powers were locked in terrible combat, until the
Mongol myth of invincibility was shattered at the
Battle of Ain Jalut in 1260. Moslem leadership then
fell into the cruel hands of Baibars, Sultan of Egypt.

Atrocity after atrocity was committed as his shadow darkened over the war-torn Holy Land. An Eighth Crusade, in 1270, attempted to advance via Tunis and Egypt, but it collapsed in miserable failure.

It did not take long for the Moslems to reconquer all the Crusader lands. After two momentous centuries, the Crusade era had ended.

Left The soldiers of the Fourth Crusade ruthlessly massacre the inhabitants of Constantinople. But by the end of the thirteenth century the Moslems had driven the Christians from the Holy Land (*above*).

79

The end of the Crusades

After 1270, a number of other expeditions to the Holy Land were undertaken, but none really deserved the title of "Crusade."

As late as 1443, men took part in an expedition known today as the "Last Crusade." This was led by King Ladislas of Poland and Hungary, and his general, Nunyad. It failed, however, when the Venetians broke their promise to sail the army from Varna, on the Black Sea, to Constantinople. A Turkish army defeated the Crusaders at Varna.

The "Children's Crusade" was the most pathetic expedition of all. A twelve year-old French peasant boy, Stephen of Cloyes, had shown King Philip a letter which bid him organize an expedition to Jerusalem. The boy claimed it had been sent to him by Christ himself. Philip refused to listen, but Pope Innocent III supported this youthful leader: "The very children put us to shame," he cried. And in the summer of 1212, about thirty thousand excited French boys and girls set off in the direction of the Holy Land – without any proper equipment or food.

Many starved even before they reached Marseilles. And there they found that the sea would not roll back as Stephen had promised. Instead, two merchants offered to sail the young Crusaders to Palestine, free of charge. Stephen believed that God had sent him these two men, Hugh the Iron and William the Pig. But the merchants had other reasons for helping. They sailed their helpless victims not to the Holy Land but to the Saracen port of Bougie, in Algeria. There the boys and girls were sold into slavery. Some were beheaded for refusing to become Moslems. Only one member of the Crusade, a young priest, is known to have returned home – after eighteen years of slavery.

While Stephen's Crusade was meeting its tragic fate, another movement had begun in Germany. A young boy, Nicholas, also claimed to have been told by God to lead a Crusade, and twenty thousand children set out enthusiastically on their journey. This band managed to struggle over the Alps and arrived in Italy, ragged and totally exhausted. But when they reached Rome, they were turned away – and only two thousand survived the journey home.

Left Hundreds of excited children – shoving, jostling and singing hymns – set out in the summer of 1212 to fight the Infidel in the Holy Land. Few of them ever returned.

5. Reasons and results

The terrible episode of the Children's Crusade is in sharp contrast to earlier crusading zeal. At the end of the eleventh century, knights, princes and peasants had all "taken up the Cross," even though their reasons for doing so were extremely mixed.

But soon, most people preferred to leave the crusading to others. Ordinary men became weary of the idea. Peasants quickly realized that only kings and noblemen returned after a defeat. Ransoms were paid to ensure their safety, but the common soldiers were left to suffer torture and death.

Moreover, taxes had to be levied to pay this ransom money, and to finance the expeditions to the East. Crusaders often pawned their lands in order to pay for their adventures. But stricter creditors at home demanded rents, and caused added hardship for the tenants.

While landowners and rulers were away, affairs at home fell into confusion. This was especially true during the reign of King Richard I in England. People began to curse the Crusades, and to stand aside when appeals for recruits were made, even preferring that children should take their place.

Popular support was dwindling. Yet equally important in bringing about the end of the Crusade era was the failure of those who led the expeditions to work amicably together. Dissension hindered efficient military planning and rapid, decisive action.

Furthermore, the Moslems had the advantage of being permanently in the area. The disunited Crusaders, on the other hand, came and went. Military successes against the Moslems could not efficiently be followed up.

Finally, in the mighty clash between Saracen and Mongol, the Crusaders found themselves caught in a vice between two forces, and were unable to cope.

Left An impressive statue of the glorious Crusader king, Richard the Lionheart, stands outside the House of Lords. Yet during his reign Richard imposed crushing burdens on his subjects. The women were left to till the land (*above*), and the affairs of state fell into confusion.

Military lessons

The failure of the Crusades did not diminish their effect upon the future of Western Europe. They had a tremendous and far-reaching impact.

The first Crusaders journeyed to the Holy Land to defeat the "barbaric heathens," and they were shocked to find that they themselves were in many respects far more barbaric. Ordinary men like Rolf came home to pass on this discovery.

Then, for the next two centuries, three different kinds of people met in close conflict: the western Christians, the Byzantines, and the Moslems. In spite of the hostilities between these three groups, there was a spreading and intermingling of ideas and customs. Each learned something from the other. The Crusaders profited most, because they had the most to learn. This was especially true in the case of tactics and military efficiency.

During the First Crusade the Moslem's military skill frequently proved superior to that of the Crusaders. The capture of Jerusalem and the success of the Crusade were not due to any superior western tactics but rather to division among the Moslem forces.

Left Crusaders learned a lot from the elaborate and advanced castles in the East, and brought home with them new designs for towers, bastions and ditches, which led to a revolution in European castle construction.

Thereafter, the Crusaders changed their military methods to match and overcome those of the enemy. These developments included improvements in the existing rigid methods of fighting a battle by employing light cavalry and infantry, and encouraging close cooperation between them.

Crusaders learned even more from the other major form of military clash, the siege. Previously, "castles" in northern Europe had been plain wooden fortresses on the summit of hills. Now, Crusaders experienced the elaborate and advanced castles in the East, with towers, bastions, ditches and a host of other defensive ideas.

The Crusaders took over these castles, and copied them when building frontier posts in the Holy Land. Krak des Chevaliers, in Tripoli, is a typical example of a Crusader castle. Designs were brought home, and resulted in a revolution in European castle construction and city defence in the twelfth century. Many of these castles and city walls still stand today as solid reminders of the expeditions to the Holy Land.

Taste of the East

As ordinary men like Rolf returned from the Crusades, they brought back with them new words, such as damask, sofa, mattress, tariff, bazaar, and magazine. And Europe gained not only the words, but all that they represented. It was during the crusading era that cotton was first seen in Europe. With it came cotton paper, an Arab invention, which took the place of expensive parchment. This made possible an increase in the production of books, with tremendous consequences for teaching and culture.

Other imports from the East included cloth, and a variety of spices -- cloves, nutmeg, cinnamon, musk and mace. Sugar became known to thousands of people, together with apricots, lemons, damsons and melons. Food became more exciting, and meals more like those we eat today.

Homes were able to be infinitely more comfortable, especially for those who could afford the new carpets and tapestries. Clothing became more exotic. Turbans were popular for a while, and slippers, unknown till then, came to stay. Women used cosmetics, and admired themselves in another innovation, the glass mirror.

Scholars learned other Eastern secrets, and carried them home. Moslems had developed mathematics, and by the twelfth century they had made startling progress in optical science. This led to the invention of the telescope, and the discovery of a completely new world.

Medical learning proved even more impressive. Arabs had separated numerous chemicals, such as potassium, silver nitrate, nitric and sulphuric acid. They used drugs in hospital operations, and had

86

studied questions of hygiene, drainage and soil irrigation.

The Moslems were also masters in the art of metalwork, using silver, gold, bronze, copper, iron and steel to make a host of items, from cooking utensils to weapons.

Merchants, scholars, travellers and soldiers brought back a long list of lessons which they had learned in the East, and which they could then teach or sell to others. And the Moslems were the people whom the Crusaders had first judged barbaric!

Above The Moslems were far more advanced in science and medicine than the Europeans, and many of their practices were taken back to Europe by the returning Crusaders.
Left This wooden and ivory panel covered a prayer book belonging to King Baldwin of Jerusalem.

The legacy

When one considers all these changes brought about or accelerated by the Crusades, it soon becomes clear that the expeditions to the East had far more than military value. They should not be seen merely in terms of knights in armour, Richard the Lionheart, Saladin, massive battles and cruel slaughter. The Crusades represented a coming together of peoples. And benefits were as much cultural and social as they were military.

Even the knight in armour emerged considerably different. At the beginning of the Crusades, the knight was far from being the proud, dashing figure of later history. He was more likely to be a petty noble, embarking upon the Crusades to satisfy his lust for adventure and his personal greed.

Gradually, however, a change took place. The knightly orders of the Hospitallers and the Templars were created. Despite their numerous faults and their eventual destruction, these organizations helped to give birth to a type of knighthood, which came much nearer to the Romantic version.

Ideals of noble chivalry began to grow after the Crusades. Poets began to sing of heroic love. The desire to please a lady became a greater motivation for brave deeds than the desire to please the King or the Church – even though the lady in question might be another man's wife. Knighthood had shed some though not all of its former squalor. So too had the western world as a whole.

The eastern influence ushered in by the Crusades allowed Europe to shed the last thick mantle of the Dark Ages. The way ahead seemed bright and full of promise.

Left The Crusades helped to introduce into medieval life new concepts of chivalry and honour, typified by the noble knight of romance and legend.

Table of dates

570 Birth of Mohammed, and the start of the Moslem religion.

638 Saracens occupy Jerusalem.

1076 Seljuk Turks seize Jerusalem. Massacre of Christians.

1095 Council of Clermont. Pope Urban II appeals for a Crusade to the Holy Land (November).

1096 The People's Crusade, led by Peter the Hermit, ends in disaster (April–October).
Start of the First Crusade (August).

1097 Siege and capture of Nicaea (May–June).
Battle of Dorylaeum, and defeat of the Turks (1st July).
Siege of Antioch begins (21st October).

1098 Antioch captured by the Crusaders (3rd June).
Crusaders in turn trapped in Antioch by a large Turkish army under Kerboga (5th June).
The finding of the Holy Lance, and the defeat of the Turks besieging Antioch (28th June).

1099 Siege of Jerusalem by the First Crusade (9th June–18th July). Its capture results in terrible slaughter of the inhabitants.
Battle of Ascalon marks the end of the First Crusade (12th August).

1144 The Turks under Zangi seize the Crusader state of Edessa.

1147 Start of the Second Crusade.

1148 Crusaders capture Damascus, but disagreement between its leaders ends the campaign.

1169 Saladin becomes Saracen leader.

1187 Saladin defeats Christians at Hattin (4th July).
Saladin invades Palestine (June).
Capture of Jerusalem by Saladin (2nd October).

1189 Start of the Third Crusade.

1191 Richard I, the Lionheart, lands at Acre (8th June).
Capture of Acre by the Crusaders (12th July).
Battle of Arsuf; Richard I defeats Saladin (7th September).

1192	Richard I marches on Jerusalem. Treaty concluded between Richard and Saladin (2nd September). Richard and the Crusaders return home to Europe.
1193	Death of Saladin. The break-up of his empire affords the Christians a breathing space.
1200	The Fourth Crusade is launched.
1204	The capture of Constantinople by the Crusaders marks the end of the Fourth Crusade (April).
1215	Start of the Fifth Crusade.
1221	Fifth Crusade is defeated by the Moslems even before it reaches the Holy Land.
1228	The Sixth Crusade is launched.
1229	Crusaders under Frederick II of Germany successfully bargain for Jerusalem, and a land corridor to the coast.
1243	Mongols seize Anatolia.
1244	Persians fleeing from the Mongols capture Jerusalem from the Crusaders.
1248	Launch of the Seventh Crusade in an attempt to regain control of Jerusalem.
1250	Seventh Crusade defeated by the Egyptian Moslems.
1260	Defeat of the Mongols at the Battle of Ain Jalut. Moslems under the Egyptian Sultan Baibars gain in power.
1271	Capture of the Crusader stronghold of Krak des Chevaliers by Baibars.
1291	The fall of Acre, the last Crusader foothold in the East.

Glossary

ABBASID An Arab tribe renowned for its cruelty, which seized power in 749 A.D., and established its capital at Baghdad.

ASSASSINS A group of Moslem fanatics founded by the Persian Hasan as-Sabath in the eleventh century. They lived in mountain strongholds, and would sweep down to murder their opponents. They were finally defeated by the Mongols in 1256.

BASTION Part of a castle wall which projects outwards to give added firepower.

BYZANTINE Term used to describe the eastern Roman Empire, centred on Constantinople (or Byzantium).

CHAUSSES Thick stockings criss-crossed with leather, which were often worn by knights.

FEUDAL A system of society based on the leasing of land to tenants in return for services as well as payment – conditions which often amounted to slavery for the tenant farmers.

FRANKS. Originally the name of the Germanic people who conquered Gaul in the 6th century A.D.; hence the word France.

GREEK FIRE An explosive liquid made from asphalt, petroleum, sulphur and other chemicals, which was fired at the enemy from copper tubes.

HALBERD A combined spear and battle-axe.

HAUBERK A long coat of mail.

HOSPITALLERS An order of monks, founded in 1100. Its proper name was the Knights of the Order of St. John. They were originally intended to care for pilgrims on the way to the Holy Land, but they became increasingly involved with military aspects of the Crusades.

ISLAM "The Right Way" – the Arabic term for the religion founded by Mohammed in A.D. 622. The word is also used to mean all the nations that follow that religion.

JOUST A mock combat, usually between two knights on horseback, and armed with blunted lances.

MACE A large club, with a spiked metal head.

MAIL Armour made from small metal rings or chain work (the term derives from the French word *maille*, meaning mesh).

MANGONEL A military machine something like a giant catapult, which was used for hurling stones and other missiles, especially during a siege.

MONGOL An inhabitant of Mongolia, a barren steppe land between China and Siberia.

MOSLEM A follower of the prophet Mohammed.

SARACEN A term derived from the Arabic word *Sharkeyn*, meaning Eastern. "Saracen" was used by the Crusaders to describe in general terms the Moslem enemy in the Holy Land, whether they were Turks, Kurds, Arabs, Egyptians or Persians.

SCIMITAR An Oriental sword of curved steel, which broadens out towards the point.

TEMPLARS A religious knightly order founded in about 1118 on the same lines as the Hospitallers. Their uniform was a red cross on a white background.

TOURNAMENT A display in which teams of armed men on horseback competed against each other for prize money.

TREBUCHET A siege engine used for throwing stones. It had a long pivoting arm, with a massive weight at one end.

Further Reading

Belloc, H., *The Crusades: the World's Debate* (Cassell, 1937) – deals mainly with the important First Crusade and its immediate aftermath; very worthwhile.

Buehr, W., *The Crusaders* (Putnam, 1959) – a straightforward account of the Crusades, and what they achieved.

Hindley, G., *Medieval Warfare* (Wayland, 1971) – a survey of European warfare from 600 to 1500 A.D. with many illustrations.

Kerr, A. J., *The Crusades* (Wheaton, 1966) – a good, fast-moving account of the Crusades from their beginnings in the seeds of discord sown by the growth of Islam.

Oakeshott, E., *A Knight and his Armour* (Lutterworth Press, 1970) – a clearly illustrated narrative about the armour which was so important to medieval fighting men.

Sutcliffe, R., *Knight Crusader* (Oxford, 1971) – an exciting tale of a boy's adventures in the Holy Land, by an outstanding historical writer.

Sorley Walker, *Saladin* (Dobson, 1971) – an excellent review of the Moslems' greatest leader – Saladin. It is interesting to see the Third Crusade – Richard the Lionheart's Crusade – through the eyes of the other side.

Treece, H., *The Crusades* (Bodley Head, 1962) – an extremely readable, comprehensive and accurate introduction to this complex period.

Index

Picture Credits

The author and publishers wish to thank all those who have given permission for copyright photographs to appear as illustrations on the following pages: Radio Times Hulton Picture Library, *frontispiece, jacket (back)*, 8–9, 10, 14–15, 20–21, 24–25, 29, 30, 32–33, 40, 43 (left), 46–47, 48, 52, 53, 56–57, 62–63, 66–67, 69, 70, 74–75 (bottom), 78–79, 80–81, 82–83, 84–85, 86–87; the Mansell Collection, 11, 16–17, 18–19, 28, 34–35, 38, 43 (right), 45, 50, 64, 65, 89; Trustees of British Museum, *jacket* (front), 12–13, 23, 26–27, 36–37, 54, 58–59, 61, 72, 74–75 (top), 79; Victoria and Albert Museum, 68; Bibliothèque Nationale, 76.
The drawings were done by John Walters.